THE TRUTH I DIDN'T TELL

Overcoming through the Power of Reflection

Recondius Obrien

Copyright © 2020 Recondius Obrien

All rights reserved. No part of this publication may be reproduced, distributed, or transmitted in any form or by any means, including photocopying, recording, or other electronic or mechanical methods, without the prior written permission of the Publisher, except in the case of brief quotations embodied in critical reviews and certain other noncommercial uses permitted by copyright law. For permission requests, write to the author, addressed "Attention: Permissions Coordinator," at the address below.

Recondius Obrien
Recondiustheauthor@gmail.com
www.theoexperience.com

ISBN-13: 978-0-578-77574-6

Publishing Coordination Services & Cover Design By
ThriveHer Publishing House

DEDICATION

Dear Reader,

I hope that as you unlock the gates to which you have held your truths hostage that you never ever allow your voice to be silenced again. You now hold the keys to your unlocked destiny.

Heddie,
The power in your truth is remarkable! The sound of your truth will continue to change lives! Thank you for loving me!
Deondrub O'Brien

CONTENTS

Dedication iii
Preface v
Acknowledgments vii

1. Sissy 1
2. Shame 13
3. Forgiveness 21
4. Resentment 29
5. Stained Glass windows 37
6. Daddy 46
7. PTSD 57
8. Superman 67
9. The Day After Superman 75
10. Tumor 83
11. Be Patient with Me 91
12. Love… 99
13. Brokenhearted 105
14. Growing Pains 115
15. Free 125
16. Blues Dancing 129

About the Author 137

PREFACE

"The Truth I Didn't Tell..." is an intricate narrative that was the catalyst in my emergence as a whole human being. In many ways it saved my life because I had no place else to turn. What began, as journal entries to release pinned up aggression and energy became pieces that I would often refer back to in times of despair? My truths shared with others became life rafts in their own storms. It was then that I knew there was more to this story.

Deciding to create a book from these very personal entries made me more vulnerable than I was comfortable with. However, I wasn't comfortable not telling the truths that may help someone else who didn't have the courage or strength to overcome.

Being vulnerable about life experiences can create portals for judgement and while that's not mine to manage, I did not want to set myself up for the scrutiny or the judgement of those that have had an inside glimpse of my life.

The good news is that I have already overcome the obstacles from the oppression of people.

The groundwork was already there however having to go back to the place of uncertainty, abandonment, pain and love were the more difficult parts to access. I dreaded having to revisit those areas uncertain of its impact upon my tender psyche. Uncovering the graves that I had so carefully buried would it cause me to mourn again? Would I resort back to the person I was prior to my exploration? I wasn't sure but I had to take the chance.

I am most happy that I did because "The Truth I Didn't Tell" will now be used as a reference of how to take your power back by telling your own truth. Now I am giving access... keys to the places that grew me.

ACKNOWLEDGMENTS

Writing has always been my therapy and this book was indeed cathartic. Although this book is not solely based on my childhood as much as it is about my development from a child into the man you see today. Writing gave me a safe place to be vulnerable while I released so many of the unresolved feelings that I tried to forget.

So I would like to especially give thanks to God for the mental strength to push through to completion. There were days when I was not sure if I could be so transparent but I was able to and it feels good to shed the weight of yesterday.

I would like to thank my mother and father for creating me out of their love. It was because of my mother's strength and tenacity that I learned survival and it was my father's quiet strength that gave me the grace to endure. I am because they allowed me to be.

Thank you "love" for showing me your beauty and your pain. It taught me how to be unconditional with my expectations.

Additionally I would like to thank my friends that gave me a safe space to share some of my journal entries in an effort to see if there was substance to create a book. Many of you gave me your honest, unadulterated thoughts and that helped me to become a better writer.

To the many persons who counted me out... Thank You! I made it and because of you I am a living, breathing testimony.

Navigating through this thing called life is a daily learning process and while I am still growing with it; I am grateful to have been trusted with chaos!

While the picture isn't quite complete and it is still being painted; I am grateful for the scars… They show just how beautiful the end result will be.

...Somehow I thought if I reintroduced my unadulterated self to the world then... they would accept me.

1
SISSY

Dear Journal,

I remember that Easter Sunday morning when I found out that I was different from other children. I was maybe three years old and Mommy had dressed me in my Easter's finest as if I were about to deliver my best Easter speech. She went all out for me to be perfect. My hair was freshly pressed and there I sat looking like a little James Brown and you told me to "sit down and don't move until it is time to go..."

As I sat there trying to emulate the perfect child; I overheard our cousin say to my mother... "He's too pretty to be a boy; you're going to turn him into a sissy." I didn't know what a 'Sissy' was or even what one looked like, but that seed was planted into my spirit that day.

As children do, I began to look for what I was 'supposed' to become. That one sentence would change my life forever.

The irony about that completely innocent day is that someone imposed her insecurity onto me and it tainted my mind to believe that something was wrong with me. I was too young to know the depth of what she was saying; but I knew at that moment I began to question if I were really different. I overheard an adult conversation that implied that something was wrong with me. What I know now is that small idea embedded itself into my brain causing much confusion as I began to try to search for answers. Its seed grew to muddle my thoughts of security into thoughts of insecurity. The idea that I should know confidence instead I was lead to question so many things about myself.

The search for acceptance in a world that seemed hell bent on misunderstanding me... thus began. I really didn't know that the seed that was planted into my young mind that Easter morning would fuel many of my choices and decisions.

Mommy was so covetous and protective of me. She began teaching me early to be responsible and disciplined. It seemed her intention was to ensure that I knew that she did the best she could by me and for me. I remember being a small person when I was put on a chair to wash the dishes. She told me then that I would not be a lazy child. Being eager to please her, I climbed onto the chair with her help and tried as I might to wash the dishes to please her. That day my childhood left as each dish that wasn't clean was put back into the sink for me to do over. I didn't want to play the 'dishes' game anymore but it was too late... the grooming had begun.

By the time I was eight or nine I was able to wash and fold clothes for the entire household and cleaning the house had become second nature. I didn't know that it was a little unusual for a child to carry that responsibility, but I was more afraid to not get it right. I did not want to disappoint her and I was careful to not make her angry. The consequences of making her angry could result in my getting my head knocked into the side of the toilet or have all of the dishes in the cabinets being taken from the cabinets for me to wash again.

I began to emulate my mother's love for hair very early. I remember climbing onto her bed and mimicking what she had done to the many friends that came to our home to get their hair pressed. Afterwards I wanted to "make her pretty" even though I remember you being the prettiest girl I had ever seen. My mother allowed herself to be my doll until my sister was born and then I took to the confines of the shadows to "fix" the dolls' hair because I thought they should look better. She would fuss at me as soon as the television light caught me and would say to me "you trying to be a Sissy?!" There was that dreadful word again threatening my existence because I still didn't know what one was. My grandfather would tell her to leave me alone because I could possibly grow up to be a renowned hairstylist. Grandfather was right; I did. But not without that word haunting me from the shadows for much of my career… "Sissy."

The love of styling hair seemed to seep from my pores, and it was obvious that it was a natural gift. As natural as it was... just as often she would remind me that she did not want a 'Sissy' doing hair in her house.

I even tried to get away from it but by then the kids in the neighborhood would ask me about braiding or styling their hair for pictures or the Friday night football game . I would often sneak to the neighbors' homes to do their hair hoping that you wouldn't catch me. When you did find out you reminded me that you was not raising no 'Sissy!!' By this time the word was like a hot sphere that would halt me dead in my tracks rendering me helpless.

The interesting thing about people though... while they may not acknowledge that I was being called a 'Sissy;' it didn't matter as long as I finished doing their hair before I went home to see if punishment awaited.

I lived with that word for years and was much older when I realized that I was okay. Coming to grips that maybe there was some truth to it considering... After all I was styling hair and there was some ambiguity around my sexuality so maybe it was true.

It seemed I was finally living up to what the little boy had heard all those years ago right? At that time the only thing I loved was transforming people and their beauty.

In my innocence I expressed my talent and that talent grew into a creative outlet. I found my rhythm and a safe space to explore the thoughts running rampant in my head. It was styling hair that made me feel normal and not ambiguous.

While growing up I didn't know any details about my father; other than his name. I would ask ever so often to see if I would get a different response; I never did. So eventually I stopped asking about him because that seemed to really anger her. I was not sure why my asking created such frustration, but it felt like animosity aimed towards me. Yet it was my reality and there seemed to be nothing I could do to change that. So, I worked really hard to not think about my father or irritate her by asking about him.

Mommy's consistent answer when asked about him was, "He isn't here; you can go where he is so you can stop asking me about him!" I had no idea why the question about my father always yielded such venom until I later learned that I was a direct reflection of what had been loss. His departure and the failed love of her life seemed to exacerbate the resentment towards me. My father was gone and here I was... his reflection reminding her of one more thing that was lost. So not only was I possibly a 'sissy' but I was the constant reminder of the repeated breaking of her heart.

So much about that dynamic shaped my life before I was old enough to be aware of how to manage it.

When my grandmother passed I was told that she had passed away; my first question was "is my father here?" She replied, "I guess... they should all be there."

That day I actually laid my now adult eyes into the same eyes that belonged to my father. The man who had been a mystery up until that point finally had a face to go with his name. This was in 1989 and a few short weeks before my high school graduation.

Now... I know that Mommy wasn't totally aware of the pain that was being inflicted upon me each time it was said, "I should've aborted you!" Every time a hand was lifted to strike me out of her frustration; it wasn't me as much as it was the reminder that I remained when her heartbeat had left with my father.

Each time I was struck I wasn't sure if that would be the blow that would send me to the hospital or the grave. However, I learned to brace myself to prepare for the onslaught of blows and words that were to come because of the seeming anger towards me.

I always felt as if I was something she regretted, and it caused me to want to be invisible. I kept trying to find different ways to please her and my efforts went unnoticed.

I even attempted to do well in school and make good grades to make her proud of me and those efforts were seen as what I was supposed to do. I don't think I knew she was proud until I was an adult and she came to visit me in NYC and told me so. I wanted her to 'like' me more than anything but that seemed to be impossible also. When I finally heard that she was proud of me it should have mattered then but it didn't. I no longer needed it because by then my life was shaped as it was. To make her 'like' me felt like energy that was wasted and I felt unsuccessful in my efforts. So eventually I left at sixteen while she shopped for groceries... for fear that what felt like hate would eventually kill me.

The Truth I Didn't Tell...

I was an adult when I made the decision that I needed closure in an effort to stop the hemorrhaging in my heart that had begun many years ago. I mulled over if I should have a conversation with my mother. Would it be worth it? Would she care? I wasn't sure because it was never mentioned even in the subtlest of ways... and after laying with the pain for longer than I can remember. I made the decision.

I called my mother one spring day after I had been in Atlanta for a little over a year to discuss the hurt; the abuse; the verbal assault and why I was resented so... the conversation was turned back to me and declared I had been given what I deserved.

In that moment I remembered the last time that I was hurt with your fist that early New Years morning of 1988. I saw flashes that took me back to the many sleepless nights prior to me leaving where I wanted to die. There were days where I merely floated through without destination not knowing where I was going or who I belonged to. I just wanted to keep moving to keep running from the reality. I didn't want to stop for fear that my reality would catch up with me. I did everything in my human power to outrun that pain. There was no real escape because no matter how much I wanted it to not be real... it was. I was there; I experienced it. I lived thru it. I am no longer in that place. Yet there I was wanting and needing the reason(s) so I could really move past that hurt.

Even though it was with the words and not the hands this time... I then understood. I had to make up my mind that I could forgive the acts without her consent. I no longer needed permission or approval to move forward but I had to do this for me. I had to face that hurt; own it and then dismantle its power over my life. The need to be heard was not as important as much as I needed for her to feel my intention.

This time it was about me. This time it was about taking my power back and knowing that I was enough. This was about a decision to move forward progressively and healthy. This was about my need to look in the mirror and see value in me; your creation. I was not a mistake and finally I understood that forgiveness was for me and not her.

This realization allowed me to escape the mental prison that kept reappearing in my life. Each time I gave my love, I would be hopeful that it would be requited; I was desperately searching for something… something that wasn't being fulfilled.

The longing I felt was for the love of my mother... I needed her. The nurturing I searched for was from the one who could right my wrongs. It was my Mom or Mommy, the woman who gave me life that I wanted and needed more than the air I breathed. I needed her more than the desire to be right.

I chose to do the work for me ideally, but I also chose her because she was my Mommy. Now my work is to love her every day and to be an example of unconditional love to her. I am stronger and better because of it. I hope those efforts can now be appreciated. After all it was done from my soul and not from my broken heart…

* Your word may not have been Sissy as mine was. However, were you ever called a name that both confused and hurt you? Causing your life to take a different turn, causing it to never be the same?

Recondius Obrien

"...unbow your head child;
the weight you carry is not yours to hold."

2
SHAME

Dear Journal,

Shame was a gift that was given to me and it haunted me just like the word "sissy." I was young and impressionable so really, I had nothing to be ashamed of. Yet somehow, I understood if I stayed out of everyone's way, I could not become who they said I was. I carried this gift of shame without reservation from place to place for fear they too would see it. I never wanted to bring unwanted attention. I simply wanted to be accepted. The irony as I look back on it is that my innocence was taken by someone else's observation of what I began to wear as my cloak. Me, not knowing any better I slipped on the shame and we became one.

We did not have a car, so I recall walking a lot. I remember those days clearly because it seemed it was Mommy and me against the world. As we walked, I would constantly walk with my head down and Mommy would pop me in the back of my head and command me to hold my head up before I walked into something. I would snatch my head up at the sting of her stern pop and would keep it up for a few minutes before the need to escape returned. It was something about the cracks of the sidewalk that pulled on me and once again I would be enthralled with something down there all over again. That's where I'd stay until I felt the sting of the next pop.

I was not aware of the feel of shame until I actually felt its cold shoulder. Shames sorrow was daunting as it seeped into my bones and made me familiar with its chilly demeanor. I cannot say that I ever wanted to be intimate with shame. But what 'they' said and what I overheard made its presence seem bigger than me. I accepted it as simply what was. It taught me very early to be seen and not heard. I learned to navigate shames dance so that way no one would have to be concerned with the sashay and sway of little ol' sissy me.

As I began to get older, I would shy away from the other kids for fear that I would not fit in and they would "see" me too. I was very guarded and careful to not bring unnecessary attention to myself. I would do creative things like sketching, reading and hair in an effort to escape the scrutiny and stay under the radar.

I remember one day on the school bus one of my neighborhood friends thought it'd be cool to pull down my pants to see how much I had "developed." They quickly discovered that I was a late bloomer. I was so embarrassed because I already didn't feel like one of the cool kids and I only really fit in with the girls. Here shame was again front and center with an entire bus load of children that witnessed my embarrassment.

I remember slowly walking home that day feeling incredibly violated and extremely vulnerable. I felt raw and exposed and afraid of what would happen when it was time to show up for school the next day. This reduced me further into my shell and made me feel even more alienated in my young psyche.

Now that I was very familiar with the weight of the shame, I could feel its grip threatening to smother me. Eventually I became an adult that had learned how to mask and manage my shame well. It had become a way of life for me and just like that kid I found myself wanting to disappear. It became very difficult to remain grounded and present even as an adult.

It took years and a lot of work for me to finally release the shame that was not ever mine. I had begun styling hair and working in a salon by the time I was sixteen. I just wanted to style hair because it came easy for me. I never expected for it to change my life. At one point I recall questioning my clients real need for me because I was not used to this. Slowly I began to see the value that I added to other people's lives and that gave me courage. I was able to now hold my head up because of the applause of my clients. However, that was just the tip of this thing that had crippled me for much of my life.

As my career grew, I found shelter from the cruel scrutiny of others in my work. I was now one of the cool kids. People saw my gift and not my shame finally... or so I thought. There I was still hiding in an attempt to not be fully seen. But I was a person who was not shown a lot of love growing up, instead I was taught survival. So, I didn't know how to acknowledge or own those feelings and needs. I found myself looking to fix others' problems because it validated my need to feel just as important as my projects. However, it was hard to understand that I was still longing to be accepted by others. What I didn't know was that it would spill over into other areas of my life.

The need for validation was and still is very real and I had no idea that I was the only person who could truly validate me. That was all that mattered to feel like who I was mattered to someone.

I did not get this revelation until I began doing my soul work. I had to learn to like the person I saw in the mirror. I had to know for myself that I was a good person and see that I was already worthy and already deserving. I had to begin to see what was already there and to appreciate the gift I was.

This wasn't a one-day realization... it remains a constant work progressing along the way. You have to remind yourself to hold your own head up. You have to square your shoulders back; take a deep breath and understand your "why." The 'why' is where it all makes sense? It is there that you can find strength to keep going in spite of what it looks like. If it were not for the 'why' I am not sure I could. What I know for sure is that there are still some days where I still want to disappear but it's a part of the journey to remain while releasing the shame. Afterall it was never my shame to begin with and I do not want it.

* Take a deep breath and think about the depth of shames effect on your life. How did shame manage to shape the rest of your life?

The Truth I Didn't Tell...

"I've heard that forgiveness was more for me than the person who offended me."

3
FORGIVENESS

Dear Journal,

Let me tell you about the irony of going through emotional trauma. It takes you on a ride that will have you blaming yourself for the actions of others. I took that ride and owned the curves and the dips of danger that lied ahead. I sincerely took ownership because I felt that it was what I was supposed to do. Even in its absence you wonder what could you have possibly done for certain things to be projected onto you. You end up questioning if they were right in the way they treated you. I am not certain if being an empath had something to do with that or just the inability to not take ownership of someone else's stuff. I spent many years attempting to outrun what was projected onto me and it was exhausting running from stuff. It seemed as if every attempt was made to quiet or still the sound of my voice... the sad part is that it almost worked.

Unlearning; relearning; accepting and dispelling that which isn't yours can feel like an uphill battle. And in many ways, it is because when you are young and impressionable you soak most things in and hold them sacred to your own beliefs. Many times, you find yourself questioning what you have heard and even refuting it because of the uncertainty of its truth. It's not until you realize that this is yet another thing that is not yours to begin with as you try to unravel the web of manipulation. In the process of unlearning I became frustrated with myself for being so weak and vulnerable. In that same space I have learned how to forgive myself for what I simply did not know.

My process to forgiveness was long and complicated. There were twists and turns that created valley lows and mountain peaks as you try to undo someone else's debris. It often feels heavy and weighted as you begin the process to allow your train of thought to be redirected to what works for you. Learning to forgive myself has been just as hard as all of the other things that I adapted as my own. However, forgiveness I actually wanted; moreover, needed in order to begin my wellness journey.

As I navigated thru the folds and bends of forgiveness; I had to first acknowledge that a wrong had occurred. Once you acknowledge that something(s) has transpired to cause you discomfort or given you reason to question yourself… it becomes very real. In some ways it can suggest that you have not been one hundred percent authentic with yourself.

Then begins the process of taking ownership… which is where I have struggled the most. Why is it my responsibility to undo something that someone else has done? For me it's actually the hardest part to beginning the forgiveness piece. The desire to not place blame and understand that forgiveness is more about my need than it is for the aggressor. That has been the best part of understanding it from a different perspective.

To comprehend that forgiveness does not require an explanation for the damage done to me was huge. For a very long time I expected apologies and reasoning for the unnecessary hurt that was projected onto me. The thing about that is that many times those projections came from a personal place of pain and insecurity... and those apologies never came. And to be honest I stopped expecting them. Once I took ownership of my reaction, I was able to begin the process of forgiving them and myself.

Removing that pressure provided me with the ability to see things differently. Additionally, I was empowered to take my power back! I no longer felt the need to take on someone else's projections unless I chose to. I began understanding also the power to disagree with something that did not suit me. I did not have to allow the imposition of someone's opinion into my psyche. Being able to finally chart my destiny as I saw fit empowered me greatly. I not only forgave the persons for their indiscretions but I also forgave me.

To say that forgiveness is a constant work is a huge understatement. While its rewards are liberating it is quite easy to resort back to what is familiar. So, I forgave me for being a victim. I forgave me for remaining a victim. I forgave me for not choosing a different means of handling my insecurities. Moreover, I forgave the little person inside of me that still expected an apology and blamed me for not standing up for what was best for both of us. He nor I chose our existence nor our destiny, but we could change how the story would end. I stopped listening to the narrative of others and I begin rewriting how I wanted to view my life. Those things grew me; empowered me and threatened to stretch me beyond what I reasoned was enough. Additionally, inside of me was the strength to understand the crippling power of un-forgiveness.

    Prayer, daily affirmations as well as the respect of persons that desire to know your choices are a few things that helped me to remain strong. As the adage goes adding pressure creates diamonds and adding weight makes a person stronger. So, as I continue to grow, I am strengthened, and I am reminded of the grace required to forgive myself for simply not knowing what I did not know. I am now the illustrator of my masterpiece and forgiveness was my brush.

* As hard as the indiscretion may have been it is actually that much harder to forgive. Think about the last time someone offended you willingly and unknowingly. Where did you find the grace to forgive?

Recondius Obrien

"... Holding on to the anger is easier than letting go. Or is it?"

4
RESENTMENT

Dear Journal,

I had two younger siblings that grew up in the same house as me. I was the eldest as well as the only boy. My two sisters were left in my care a great deal of the time and I tried to take good care of them. I was able to practice my craft on them and they became my personal dolls. My desire to be a responsible son and to be a good sibling was apparent as I took great pride in caring for my sisters. But I also wanted to finally make my mother proud of me by taking care of home as she left me in charge. My role as big brother was a big deal. I helped with homework; ironed school clothes and did their hair for school. I took that responsibility seriously as their older sibling.

My baby sister was easy because she really looked up to me. She pretty much followed me around and I loved doting on her. I do not think to date that we ever had a misunderstanding. There is a ten-year difference between she and I and a five-year difference with my middle sister. My relationship with my mothers second born was not easy from day one for some reason. Even when it was just the two of us, there seemed to always be some tension of some sort that kept us at odds. Her resentment provoked her to do unmentionable things in hopes of getting back at me. Now don't get me wrong I am aware that siblings' bicker and fight sometimes, but her obvious resentment towards me seemed to be ever growing. Even though I was the one who was left to care for her, to help and protect her, she stayed quite resistant to my efforts.

My younger sisters' presence caused great resentment from my middle sister and it only seemed to intensify, as her disdain grew more apparent. It seemed that if the attention was not solely on her there were always problems to follow. As children you don't really think of how your siblings' actions towards you can affect you emotionally but trust me they can. There were no limits to what she would or would not do to keep the attention on her. At some point I stopped caring to be honest. My goal was to be invisible and to a point I was. That was until she began to use that same resentment to get me in trouble with my parents. I received many punishments as a result of her intentional lies and devious behavior. I eventually grew numb to her divisiveness, but I became guarded with her. I just awaited the next assault to hit. In a million years, I did not think that I could have a sibling that could harbor that much ill will towards me. But I did.

As we grew older and I left home I did not have to deal with it directly unless it affected my mother and father. And yes, there were many times I was summoned to deal with her and the reckless behavior. Most times I was successful in diffusing the storm that had become her but the times I was not present were not very nice.

I oftentimes found myself in the absolute fight of my life with my own sibling!!

Other times I walked into the storm hoping to be the calm needed for all involved and I would end up refereeing a verbal war of slander and vicious accusations; other times I became the targeted Imagine looking at your first sibling whom you cared for; protected and helped navigate through some of life's hardest transitions and finally realize that she resents you. That whole thought messed with my head badly and I began to blame myself for the break in our relationship. I was the eldest and supposed to be more leveraged and reasonable. Somehow I became another reason why she resented me?

At some point after too many direct attacks to count; I disassociated myself from my middle sister and I no longer allowed her actions to affect me. I was determined to stop her from hurting me with her actions, moreover her words. I think maybe because she witnessed some of my shortcomings, she knew how to say things that would cut to my heart. Hearing things like "I hate you and I wish you would die" can destroy a person. In many ways it almost did. Yet, I understood that because it was her, the words hurt worse than the devious behavior. In many ways it solidified what others had said and it became a reminder that maybe I wasn't good enough. Her words were intentionally assigned to assassinate my character. My heart bled each time we fought and each time the wedge between us grew.

I distinctly recall after my dad's funeral I experienced my final onslaught of repeated verbal attacks. It was so severe that I vowed to never place myself in the same space with her longer than necessary... if that. The things she said to me out of her resentment of me now aggravated the pain that was already obvious. I promised she and God that I would not ever allow myself to be in the line of fire from her ever again as long as I remained alive.

This post funeral altercation occurred out of disrespect for our mother. I was still grieving and processing my father's death and now this. The name calling and the jabs at my character and sexuality caused me to stop seeing my sibling. I now saw a woman who was a part of my past. The irony is that whenever I was in any proximity of her I could not help but be reminded of the hurtful things that she had said and done. I found myself never wanting to be in the same space as her for long because I could no longer trust that she would not go further to inflict injury. Eventually I made the choice to not subject myself to become more damaged by her actions. It was hard to actually do because after all she was still my sibling.

Resentment is a powerful tool and to move past its power is not an easy feat. It's a constant work to forgive the people that have used resentment to poison their own judgment.

That is what I did by choosing me; I forgave the act but I, no longer desired to be the target. Once I realized that something about me was a trigger for her; it was my responsibility to not trigger her. I had to be accountable for my own mental wellness; moreover, my healing. I was now strong enough to not allow her words and actions to break me down as they had done so many times before. Now I knew better and I knew me. There was no way she could annihilate my character when I knew the truth.

There was difficulty in not wanting to fix our relationship, but I did not break it. I can say even with the history there remains a broken space in the same place that tugged at my heartstrings. I may never know what caused any of the ill feelings that she has held against me; yet it is my job to not hold that same resentment against her. I can now be cordial and pleasant without the fear of a verbal assault. I recognize before the tide turns to get out well before the tsunami. To many that may seem cowardly but in making the choice to choose me... I don't need to stay to prove I am stronger. The days of enduring unnecessary heartaches are gone, and I pray for the patience and understanding to not repeat the cycle.

* Have you ever had to stand in the face of resentment; that face being someone you love? Where do you find the space to love someone that is jealous of you?

The Truth I Didn't Tell...

"You wanted perfection & I simply wanted the grace to be seen."

5
STAINED GLASS WINDOWS

Dear Journal,

My life as an adult changed when I decided to take my power back. While doing the work to become free from what people were imposing on me, I created a bubble where I could no longer be hurt by people and their opinions. At least that is what I told myself. I kept my head up. I put my shoulders back and I became the person that I saw myself as prosperous, respected, versed and most of all integral. I had literally stained myself away from my past with each piece of hurt and became an ideal human. The perfect stained-glass window... where you could see the beauty that was projected but you could not see the inside where the cracks lived.

There could be no shame because I left no room for error. I was careful to be well put together and present. Not one time, but every time I had to show up! Even when it took my breath away to stand, I stood. There were many times where I was accused of being difficult to work with because I was a perfectionist. However, I would no longer allow people to use me against me. I stood with my integrity and my pride intact wounded and bleeding, but no one knew that but God and me of course.

It's so interesting because in the midst of all of these new revelations about myself; I also had a head on collision with God, and at twenty-seven years old I accepted my call to ministry. I was in the process of buying my first house and it was taking forever! I had all but given up and one Sunday evening I was arrested in my car leaving a church service. I began to hear these words "I chose you and everything that you think you are; I put inside you for me to use for my glory!" I was so dumbfounded that I drove home in a daze and after arriving I laid in the floor face down and cried. Reluctantly I was able to accept that God saw me much differently than man and I believed that if He saw me unashamed maybe now I would be accepted and be a part of the "called."

What I didn't anticipate was that ministry would become shame all over again. The persons whom I wanted to trust to be my 'safe space' actually used my truth against me and used that same truth to manipulate me because they knew my heart was pure. I simply wanted to be used. It was my desire that people saw God and His transforming power inside of me. However, instead what I learned was that ministry houses a lot of manipulation and its tactics are often used to keep people under their control; including me. You see the thing about being broken and surrendering to God and leadership you actually want to learn from your mistakes. You make the decision to change and be different from your old self. What I kept finding was that there were many people hiding behind a stained-glass window.

After many years of learning how to navigate through the church stuff; I found myself back at a place that was indeed too familiar. Ashamed. Ashamed of whom I worked so hard to become. Ashamed of the work I had put in authentically to be ok. The gift of shame was unwrapped again.

The only thing that realization did was cause me to try that much harder to outrun 'their' perceptions of me. Some thought I was 'too eccentric" as I was politely told for their ministry. Others simply used my ministry gifts and my money while I sat patiently waiting to be allowed to serve in their ministry. Now don't get me wrong not every situation was bad, but it caused trust issues and certainly did not help with my already insecure, wounded self. I was not out there doing any and everything; in fact I wanted to live the life that I preached about.

Inside I knew I was a decent person however because I never shook the weight of shame, I was once again reminded of what I wasn't. I sat back, waited and watched while being manipulated. It allowed me to resort back to not feeling good enough or as if my transgressions had somehow found me. As I sat, I was able to witness a lot of the things that made me know what I didn't want to become. The idea that even in ministry you can witness deceit and practices that can make you not want any parts of church.

These stained-glass windows that I was erecting were pushing me back to the same space of separation that I felt as a child and I hated it. I hated how it felt yet because I was loyal, I remained, and I existed behind each color of the stained glass. I had no idea how to exist outside of the reality because I was not the perception that people had created for me without getting to know me. I was not what they had called me. I was answering to a different call.

How did I arrive back at the place of resistance and abandonment in the same exact place that was supposed to be my safe space? The irony in that is I had to learn that everyone in church was once in search of something. So as I began to try to understand the ministry thing I kept hoping and actually believing that what I was feeling was self-imposed until I realized that it was real and I was not making it up.

Men with their own insecurities didn't really see the call on my life nor me. What they saw was a man that was well groomed and meticulous, and they arrived at the same conclusion as the cousin so many years prior. They felt I was too 'put together' for God to truly use me so I was made to sit and serve without bringing any additional attention to myself.

I stayed hidden behind those stained-glass windows interestingly enough until I wanted to kick them in and break each one by hand. I, no longer wanted to be confined by these prisons that were being forced on me. I felt rejected and not good enough right there inside the church.

This forced me to really develop my own relationship with God. That relationship came from true intimacy in prayer and much time in worship. I could worship God and leave all of my cares there without scrutiny. I could cry out to Him and He would comfort me without question. It was there that I learned how to navigate through much of the things that I felt were imposed on me out of manipulation.

After much heartache and many more heartbreaks at the hand of those that were designed to protect me. I finally said, "enough" and I made the decision to break all of the stain glassed windows that kept me hidden from living authentically. I learned to bring all parts of me into the room. I would no longer make excuses for their slights; nor would I reduce my character to make anyone else comfortable. In actuality the room would learn to adjust opposed to bringing in pieces of me with the hopes that they would allow their comfort to invite the rest of me.

Finally, I was no longer a prisoner behind all of those patterns and colors. I was able to fully show up as well as own my truth. I know who God called me to be and if He was good with it, others would learn to be also. I made the effort to show up in the true spirit of who I was... moreover who I was becoming. I no longer needed the validation of the pulpit or the persons selected to manage it. I could be just as effective in my seat where there was no need for a stage. The stage was set when I told God yes.

I was finally sure of who I was, and God made me know that He too was proud of me. I was able to allow the work I had to done to strengthen my resolve. I was able to emerge from behind all of the broken glass that was my personality and become a person in pursuit of wellness and wholeness. I kicked in those windows figuratively and now I can still walk into a room with my head up and be good with whom I've become. I, no longer have to be ashamed of my past or anything that has grown me to be a God-fearing man. I was finally free of the opinions of others while becoming sure of the man that God said I am. I emerged fully free from the scrutiny of persons who just like me are deserving of grace. Inside of everyone is something that they are not proud of but for me I cannot be imprisoned by any more stained glassed windows.

*This was a very difficult time for me. However, there was redemption! Has there ever been a time in your life when you felt that you couldn't live your authentic truth? If so, how did you take your power back?

Recondius Obrien

"...the hole in my heart can't heal because you could not stay."

6
DADDY

Dear Journal,

Let me tell you about my Daddy... Now I know you are saying "what Daddy because you haven't said much about a daddy moreover "The Daddy..."

So unbeknownst to many people I met my father for the first time that I was able to recollect was when I was eighteen years old. I was pretty much a grown man but yet still a child longing for his father. There was this unexplainable void that continually nagged me because you weren't there.

It was during Grandmothers transition that Mommy said, "your Grandmother has passed away." I immediately asked my mother "will my father be there?" She answered carefully "I'm sure." However, even then I could sense her trepidation with my newfound revelation. I instantly said, "call him!!"

My first questions when you answered were simple "do you know who this is?" He said, "my son;" I then asked, "where have you been?" He simply replied, "in New Jersey" and he chuckled his infamous laugh. It didn't take long for my dad's charming smile & the gentleness of his eyes as he looked at me with pride. That alone caused me to throw the past away and focus on our future. Our bond was instant… not that there wasn't residue from unanswered questions but simply because of the vast amount of time that had passed without contact. Nonetheless I chose my father over my pride.

So my Mother and Father thought it a good idea to begin dating the day he arrived back on North Carolina soil; and what a world wind courtship that was! So much so that he had given her two rings before the actual marriage. The day they got married…I stood as my fathers' Best Man as well as styled Mommy's hair and helped her get dressed for their ceremony.

I swear I became five (5) years old in anticipation of my parents actually being a unit again. As soon as the ceremony was over, I bolted down the aisle out of the church because I could no longer contain my emotions. Every child wants his parents to be together and to see the love and joy that created him and for God to honor my soul's request; gave me the greatest gift!!

For the first time in my life, I felt complete and a part of a unit. Thank you Daddy for honoring me/us. No one can truly understand the love a child has for his father unless you are a boy who thought he had lost out on that opportunity to know and experience a father's love. God indeed proved to be a God of second chances.

Mommy loved my father like I have never witnessed her loving anyone else. I know now that what those two shared was beyond my conception or me. Mommy even said to me "you were conceived in love." I often wondered about that but there's no denying that the love my parents shared was genuine and pure.

So that Wednesday evening on June 13th, 2012 as I was coming thru the Holland Tunnel being driven to the airport to get back to Atlanta; I received a call from Mommy, and she was extremely upset stating that you were nonresponsive. I did not know how that was possible because I had just left him two days prior and he was in good spirits. The doctor even mentioned that it was possible that he may be able to come home. I felt hopeful but I also remembered just a couple of week's prior when I surprised my Dad and came home for the weekend.

We sat on the sofa and laughed that day about any and everything while watching the basketball game. We had something special he and I. We could look at each other and finish the others thought without words. The very next morning I had to carry my dad out of the house and for the first time I saw fear in his eyes. He begged me not to drop him and I, after fortifying myself, assured him that I wouldn't. In that moment I also felt that he would not ever come back across that threshold…and he didn't.

The Truth I Didn't Tell...

Leading up to that day I held out hope that he would somehow beat Leukemia, but I also was not delusional to think that it was possible that he may not. I think I was preparing myself in the back of my mind even though my heart wanted a different outcome.

And now this... I instinctively asked to speak to him and Mommy held the phone to his ear. The words he spoke became his final words to me "I love you too son." I begged him to wait for me and he actually did. He waited and hours later I watched him take his last breath. It took all I had to not climb into the hospital bed and try to keep him with me. My heart broke into one million pieces, but I had to release him. He was my missing link because he made me whole. My dad completed my heartbeat because I had waited my whole life for him and now that I finally had him I didn't want to let go. Yet at that moment I had to be strong for Mommy and be there for everyone else and not remember that I was once again an orphan.

Three months later in late August of 2012 as I began closing the chapter of NYC; I boarded an airplane in Newark to meet the movers in Atlanta. I had merely existed since he had passed away and I finally made the decision that it was time to shut down the New York City apartment. And so... that's what happened. I went thru all of the necessary steps and navigated each part. I managed to get the apartment packed up; mostly quiet still trying to understand what my new reality was. The movers came on a Tuesday morning to load up everything and I got everything set up to meet them on the other side. What I didn't know was that night I would finally get the release I had not found.

I looked out of the window and simply spoke these words... 'Daddy are you out there?" In the moments that followed a single tear fell as I looked out into the night sky hoping for a glimpse of your smile one more time. Shortly after, I began to unravel right there on row twenty-four. I sobbed inconsolable for his death and tangible absence. It seemed that every part of me hurt for my Dad. I scrambled for a way to suppress the overflowing emotion that was slowly creeping up and out of my soul.

I was void of reason so I began composing a letter hoping to regain some composure and accept it. Accept that I had to live my life without him and know I would not ever be the same. Writing was the only way I could get control of the shattering of my heart. I wept for every part that we shared. I wanted to scream for the little boy that simply wanted his Daddy. Yet, no matter how much I cried though; he was gone, and it was final.

That night I relived our conversations leading up to his death and knowing that he wanted to stay with us made me that more sure that I could release him and know that God would eventually heal the hole I felt in my heart.

It's funny I can still hear his voice so clearly and remember the look and feel of his hands very strongly for some reason. Maybe because they always looked so much larger than life compared to mine. I tried to remember every one of your physical features when I realized that it was possible that he might leave me. I must have done a good job because I can conjure up many vivid images of him in color.

In those same moments I remembered my brother (Artez) who was a lot like my Dad also. Although he was five years younger than I, our DNA was undeniable. He and I sounded like my Dad, looked like him and both of us are/were men full of pride. I'm not sure if fashion and hygiene practices could be genetic but he and I both could clean like professionals. He even taught us how to spit shine a shoe like military men; that was our father's doing.

My brother had been violently taken away from us and now I find myself missing them both.

One day early in our discovery he stood in my bedroom door and said to me "Son I respect you and your home; you can run your home the way you see fit." That day spoke volumes about how much he respected me as a man and as his son. That gave me so much love and acceptance. Material was never anything I needed because I have always believed in hard work. What my father gave me with his approval was priceless and I can't ever say how valuable that was to me.

The pride on his face when he would walk into my establishment and stand quietly in the corner and just smile was oftentimes my greatest joy. I would look up and see him and now I realize I saw me in his eyes. The love that my Dad and I shared was so free without "stuff" and that made it so easy.

I remember the first time my dad called and said "Son, what are you doing?" I replied, "nothing man sitting here talking to my roommate." He said, "Ok I didn't want anything. I can talk at you later… I love you" without me saying it first. I hung up the phone and cried because I knew he meant it.

I smiled as I recalled "our" times; the days when he would say something on the sly and I would get it. The way we would both chuckle at our private jokes. I missed the days when he would wash my car and then cruise till he had to come and get gas money. Eventually I learned to give him extra before he left. I knew there was nothing he wouldn't do for me if it were in his power. We were easy like that.

Sometimes I feel robbed because my Dad and I only had twenty-two years of unconditional love. It seemed I waited my whole life for him to come and love me. I did ask him once if he was proud of me and he told me that he couldn't have asked for a better son. In that moment I was grateful and able to be there for him. Then cancer came and took him away from me. I feel like there was so much more love to share; so many more experiences. So much more everything...

I am not angry and I don't have any regrets. I am also not sorry for ever allowing my Dad's re-entrance into my life. Seeing his strength during his illness gave me so much pride because he wanted to fight for us. The year before he passed away he gave me so much hope just sharing stories about me as a little boy. Remembering, sharing... those are my special memories to keep.

Funny I try not to think too long about him not being here because then I may never want to get out of bed again. Yes... I have had days like that, but I don't allow them to suffocate me. I take a lot of deep breaths and inhale/exhale.

This ode to him took two months before I was able to find my voice again. It was the first thing I had written since he passed. I thought for a while that I had lost my ability to write forever. I didn't know what would come out if I tried to express what I was feeling. Nor did I want people to start with the scriptures and oil throwing (I know my Dad is laughing at that). I know who God is and that is the reason I did not lose my mind. I wanted to throw everything to hell and run for the hills BUT GOD!!! So, I had to be careful of how I shared and when I shared. I still needed time to process but this is a good start.

One thing is for sure and I am certain of is that I loved my Dad & my Daddy loved me. It was a fierce and forgiving love and I won't ever forget what it felt like to have a natural fathers love. Thank you Father (God) for the mortal man you sent to represent your love for me; my Dad... Mr. Charles Edward McCain.

* Has death ever crippled you to the point of paralysis? What was your method of release?

The Truth I Didn't Tell...

"… A soldier goes to battle for his country; I went for my heart."

7
PTSD

Dear Journal,

This week could be marked as one of the most traumatic times I have experienced in my adult life. I finally realized what was wrong with me all those times when the actions of others could pitch me into a dark abyss, and I had to crawl out of it one step at a time. Post Traumatic Stress Disorder (PTSD)… or triggers as I like to call them happen when suddenly I am jarred back to a place of trauma or pain. The rush of heat begins as a current traveling from my ankles up my body and my heart rate increases as sweat begins to pour; then my breathing becomes shallow as I fight to maintain composure. This mostly happened when something or someone spoke to me in a manner that invoked an alarm that signaled danger. Immediately I return back to the place of the personal traumas that I had experienced. The thing about a trigger is that it comes without warning and its unknown when they will occur and oftentimes, they can catch you off guard and at the most inopportune times.

I did not realize that I was a victim of PTSD until I traveled out of the country on a trip to Trinidad and Tobago for work. I was in the midst of recapping my class in preparation for the close when I began to sweat profusely; my heart rate accelerated by double or more as I slowly began to lose control. I began to take deep gulps of air attempting to calm what was happening on the inside. All the while my brain was screaming, "What the hell is happening to me?" I was praying that I would not collapse in this class of fifty plus persons. I had to hold it together… if I could.

I made it through the close of the class and after a labored attempt I was able to make it to the car. I continued to take deep breaths in an effort to calm my breathing. I allowed the air from the window to blow into my face as I tried to make sense of what was happening. As we drove up the countryside, I began to think that there was no way I could be hospitalized in a foreign country. I had to get it together. At this moment I was completely thrown off and the emotional trauma was threatening to come to the surface. Everything that I had tried to hide for a great deal of my life was now front and center.

What I know for sure was that my recent break up and the death of my father was now snowballing on me along with everything else I had managed to tuck away. I was losing control in a place I was not familiar with and I had no-one to comfort my anxiety and I was in the midst of a full-blown panic attack. It was the first of many and I had no idea how to manage a panic attack since I had never had one until now. What I did know was that if I got to my hotel, I may be able to regain control… I didn't.

After dismissing the idea that I would join the team for dinner, I went straight to my room. I looked around wide eyed remembering why I was there and seeking resolution to what was my current reality. I finally collapsed into a heap onto my bed fully dressed; clothes drenched, and I allowed myself to grieve every single thing that I had tried to manage internally for my entire life.

At that moment I lost the last remaining bit of control I had, and I allowed myself to feel every ounce of the pain that I had carried like a badge of honor forever. My thoughts time traveled back in time to the first time I felt I wasn't enough or in some cases too much. I wept for that person. My mind gave me a vivid reminder of each time I felt inadequate or not good enough. I sobbed for that person. I literally watched my life flash before my wild eyes, and I felt myself spiraling out of control even more. At that moment I grabbed something and I began to write. Writing was the only way I knew how to get through this emotional storm that I now found myself dead in the middle of. The words spilled onto the pad or device (I cannot recall) haphazardly and it was not until the next morning that I was able to make sense of it all. I was emotionally exhausted with the recurrence of the past hurts accompanied with the newer pains. PTSD had followed me all the way to another country and I still wasn't sure of what triggered it.

In those moments I came to understand that I had to acknowledge that my trauma was now posttraumatic stress disorder. I was not sure if my life would ever be the same… all I knew was last night I cried slow, silent, hot tears. My tears seemed to never stop flowing from an internal hurt deep in the recesses of my mind. I thought that I had healed or otherwise forgotten these pains. I cried for every time in my life that I haven't felt worthy or deserving of a love of my own. I cried for each time I tried to forget the hurts and heartaches that come along with rejection. Finally, I cried a soul cleansing, heart wrenching cry. I did not set out to mourn all that had happened; I just did. The more I cried, the more I began to understand that I was crying for the little boy that felt rejected and dejected because of the shape of his lips and the slant of his eyes. Moreover, I cried for every time that little boy was told he was too pretty to be a boy or that he would be a sissy because he did not like to get dirty. Yea…I cried a silent, purging cry because that little boy had become a wounded man.

I never knew that as I began to grow into that man the things that I learned, and the things said to me would leave me guarded and forlorn as it related to my own happiness. In my quest to prove every negative word and naysayer wrong, I simply forgot to live.

Brokenness can do that to your psyche. It can mess up your entire existence if you don't wrangle it and get a hold on it. It will make you accept the dysfunction as normal and normal seems foreign and farfetched. It's really crazy the irony of it all when you think about it. I am in awe of the context of this revelation in my own life. It shook me to my core that night as I sobbed for the little boy that never felt good enough to be loved completely because of the mental, physical and verbal abuse. I cried for the teenager who never fit in with his peers, so he hid behind his work because that validated him and made him feel needed.

I also mourned for the man who had become a mere wounded little boy living inside a grown man's body. He too, still wanted to fit in and be needed. He only desired to feel the true connection of someone who was capable of loving him solely without disappointment and rejection. When all you have known is conditional love it's hard to even fathom how to function with an unconditional, free, pure love…

At first, I was ashamed of my tears because it showed just how vulnerable I was. However, the more I cried the more I felt the chains being destroyed because I finally understood how parts of me have been so complete and others are fragmented pieces of what I was to become. I, then relinquished control over my emotions and I bathed in the freedom of my release. I allowed my spirit to speak truthfully to me and I was able to see how I have spent way too many years hiding behind the creative flow of my hands as a shield to my heart. My heart beat rapidly as I screamed silent, unadulterated tears into the night. The heart that had been broken and shattered for as long as I can remember poured out the pain that it has held for a lifetime. The same heart that I vowed I would protect from further abuse because it seemed that love had betrayed me was breaking again.

I didn't think I was wrong for wanting to experience the fairy tale types of love that I read and dreamt about. This was the same love that even God speaks about and desires for my life.

I even cried for the misuse of words and how they traumatized me. Sometimes I was able to outrun them; other times I could not. I learned how words could be powerful tools that were able to create beauty and destroy lives with a single utterance. I readily collected the derogatory words and somehow discarded the more complimentary words. Its funny the things the mind holds on to. Yet words used carelessly and haphazardly can leave bodies in their wake as they cut, tear, destroy and curse its target. Less often are those same words used to uplift, cheer, encourage, and bless.

Somehow in the midst of it all my heart still works; I don't know how but it still feels in spite of all my effort to shut the part that hurts off.

God is amazing like that… this healing that I thought was complete actually wasn't. They were simply scabbed over and as it was re-injured; I felt the pain that was deep, dark and dormant. His love for me would not allow me to live incomplete and I am grateful for that. He will peel back each layer carefully and once the infection is exposed then He can apply His healing power(s). His timing is perfect…

Last night I cried… for every little boy like me who had lost himself in the quest to be something or someone foreign. Only doing what he knows to do and that is survive in spite of the odds. I cried; I released, and I accepted that I am OK. I released the debt that I held against myself as well as the others that aimlessly hurt me. I cried myself to sleep hoping that my long awaited and deserved healing had finally begun.

* Triggers are very real. Where were you when you realized that your trauma was unresolved, and you had to face it in order to move forward?

The Truth I Didn't Tell…

"I don't know how people wear these masks every day; they are heavy and uncomfortable."

8
SUPERMAN

Dear Journal,

One day I found myself...buried under the heap of superhero costumes, masks, pistols, and other various weapons I have been using to save the world. All the while I lost the most important person... me. There I was in a heap underneath the facade of my life. Scarred but no longer wounded, but surely a mere shadow of the Superman that I must look like to others...

Funny, I had no idea that I even possessed this super person. Somehow, I used my own abandonment as the vein of my "Superman" strengths. Maybe I should have known that I wouldn't be able to stand by and watch others hurt as some watched me hurt. I just did what I thought I was supposed to do. Often it was done with more drive than what should have been humanly possible, but it never stopped me. Yet, it was not until I was on yet another quest to save the lost did I realize that the one who needed saving the most was me...

The mark of my realization resulted from every attempt I made to help someone else motivate towards his or her destiny, I was moving further away from my own. I sincerely lost myself in the effort to "save" the weak and downtrodden. I wanted to run in and do what I realize now had not been for me. I wanted to create a "safe" place for the lost ones with faces like mine. I wanted to give understanding to the ones who felt misunderstood and offer solace where chaos once stood. I was determined to be the voice of reason in a sea of turmoil. I simply wanted to be the one who cared; solicited or not. I wanted to be the trusted one.

It was not until the "supernatural" began to weigh heavier than the natural "human" instincts that I began to realize that something was awry. What was wrong with my letting others handle their adversity as I had been left to handle mine? Now I am not so sure that my motives were as pure as I had hoped looking at it from a different angle. Was it for them as much as I thought or was it for me...? This spoke to my need to quench the feelings of abandonment that I've felt most of my life.

The funny thing about life is that more often than not you find yourself searching for answers to questions that are subliminally asked. I don't recall ever actively seeking to be Superman. I only remember the worn-out feelings that come after I have exhausted all of my "super" powers to make life better for someone else. Its then that I've asked myself "how did I ever become involved in this anyway?"

or better yet "why do I care so much??" These questions always come but not usually until after I am too far in to really listen for an answer. Remember these questions are usually subliminal, rhetorical, even so it doesn't necessarily seek an answer.

It really was a hard pill to swallow because outside looking in… I'm whole; I'm strong. I'm resilient… or so I thought. I truly wanted to make a difference in a world that didn't even ask to be saved. I simply wanted to do for others what was never done for me.

The irony I have learned about Superman is that whenever afflicted there was literally never anyone who could come to his rescue effectively. Now I know what that feels like. Especially when you have tried to save everyone else and people seem to think you are always good; and God forbid you have a moment of weakness or vulnerability. You end up being looked upon as a weakling. This is why its important to know your weaknesses and what has the potential to weaken you. It can destroy you if you're not aware. I may have gotten it late but Thank God I get it!!

Ownership of this newfound revelation literally took my breath away. It hit me like a ton of bricks because I never knew why or how my Superman complex came to be, but it finally made sense to me. I was able to put a reason to why I am the way I am… I was merely standing in as I presumed others should have for the little boy silently crying for help. What's also profound is that you can't help or save anyone until you are able to put the oxygen mask on yourself first; this is surely a lesson learned through experience.

The day the lights came on I had feelings of shame maybe even regret because it almost felt as if I had been living a lie. There was no "Superman" and I damn sure didn't have any "super" powers but what I did have was the grace that kept me, the strength that sustained me, the wisdom to know better, and a voice that can speak boldly and with authority if I feel abandoned or assaulted.

I found myself that day buried underneath the heap of superhero costumes, masks, swords, and other paraphernalia lost under the cares of everyone and everything. Most of which had nothing to do with me but somehow that is where I was inundated with stuff that was never mine to own...today I still care but saving me is the most serious and most pressing before I save anyone else.

Superman has hung up his cape....

* Who do you become in an effort to be the person you need to be when life becomes hard?

"…What's the point of having a cape when I couldn't even save myself?"

9
THE DAY AFTER SUPERMAN

Dear Journal,

The day after I found myself buried under the heap of superhero costumes, masks, swords, pistols, shields, and weapons I had been using to save the world was a day of reckoning. Reckoning that I am not sure I ever added into my equation. It was that day that I had to take ownership of my role in wanting or needing to be Superman. As easy as the revelation came to light, I know now it would not be as easy to shed the need or desire to still rush out and save the day.

The days after the big reveal my eyes seemed to be open to a whole new world. I cannot tell you how many times I have had to reason with myself to not do more than what was asked or required. I began to look at different scenarios as they were presented, and I decided if I wanted to extend myself or not. Incidentally, the "Super" gene always stood up and it was becoming an inner fight to not allow "it" to go ahead and do what had become natural. Sincerely this thing was bigger than I ever really gave it credit. I had become so quick to "just do it," that in some scenarios the victims would just "wait for it" because why suffer unnecessarily when you know that there is someone who will save you without question?! As I began to seek out the reasoning for this superhero complex; I had feelings of weakness, misuse, abuse, and just plain humanness.

As I deduced what was happening, I saw time and time again where my help was not even warranted but I jumped in for fear that someone would drown on my watch. I had given a whole new meaning to "I am my brother's keeper?" I had always thought that the answer was a resounding "yes!!" However, this caused me to question the logic with my warped thinking. True enough I love helping but I honestly don't know if it was the need to help or the need to be validated. This led me to ask myself if I was actually helping or hiding my own vulnerability or weaknesses. Its funny the things that you learn about yourself when you are still and watch your life's movie play back.

What I was able to see now live and in 3D were holes in a life that I had filled with work and endless "super" feats to cover the gaping voids. I was using my savior complex to mask the hurt that my own life had left. Hurts that are too numerous to list but there were many. Most I had healed from, but it left me needing something to make me feel better about being vulnerable and not able to save myself. You see if you think about it...most superhero's can save most anyone. You name it burning homes, car crashes, even leaping tall buildings in a single bound, but very rarely do you see them able to save themselves. Usually that is when you see the humanistic qualities that make "super" not so super at all.

The patterns were all there. For every bruise and welt I endured, I became resilient to pain. For every unkind word, I became the voice of reason. For every shortcoming, I super imposed greatness to allow myself room for the inadequacy. In failed relationships, I would analyze and go over in my mind over and over again what I did to cause yet another relationship to end. It never occurred to me that some things just grow apart. Some things were not ever sound or meant to be but because of my inability to not look for the broken winged bird. I did not want to see the shortcomings. I reasoned in my mind that I was to accept people where they were because I myself, am not perfect. And I have learned not to expect anyone else to be. This type of thinking could have been the death of me had I not seen my "movie." I think I know why actors say they don't particularly care to watch themselves on screen, to actually see your flaws large and in living color. It is there and you do not get a do-over. Once the film has been edited and the final cut is made that then becomes a permanent part of history; I'm guessing the same goes for life...

Seeing these words unfold causes ripples to run down my spine because I realize that I was destined to a life of endless regret had my eyes not been opened. All I've ever wanted was to just live and co-exist in this life without reliving my mistakes. In essence that is exactly what I was doing, trying to fix me but through someone else. I'd replaced the victims with me; determined to not lose myself again. We eventually found out that Superman was weakened by Kryptonite. I came to reason that my Kryptonite was me. The absolute irony of it all to think that I inadvertently was holding on to hurt and rejection as if it was my job to protect it so as not to allow it to become active again. This was truly one of those things that made me go "hmmmmm..."

I had to admit my own vulnerability again when my father was diagnosed with Acute Lymphoblastic Leukemia. My mind immediately went into superhero role. I reasoned every possible scenario to fix this. I called on my peers in ministry, I prayed and cried and cried and prayed. But the still voice of my newfound revelation reminded me that this was much larger than me. I was left to my own thoughts of helplessness. I became angry and frustrated with the disease. I began to lose sleep hoping that Daddy and I could beat this. I leapt headfirst into my work trying to escape the feelings of helplessness. However, they never fully went away. In fact, the more I worked the more my mind churned into overdrive. I had to accept that this time whatever God's will was for my father, it would be done. Regardless he is the ultimate Superhero, and He has the final say. It rendered me helpless but not defeated. It also made me aware that some (if not most) battles are not mine to fight. Some things are just a part of this life and others are lessons designed to strengthen areas that are compromised.

The day(s) after Superman hung up his cape have proven to be filled with obstacle after obstacle. Each new day begged me to grab my cape and try once again to save the day. I can't because it became clarion clear that I am human and although my heart and mind say otherwise; I possess no superpowers. My fear is that this time Superman won't be able to save anyone including him.

* How hard is it not to go back to what is familiar in an effort to make yourself feel better about your own shortcomings?

The Truth I Didn't Tell...

"… They called you a silent killer;
I called you an intruder!!"

10
TUMOR

Dear Journal,

When I awakened from surgery and the doctor told me how big you were and how dangerous you looked. I wept... I couldn't understand how something that powerful could be living inside of me. Moreover, the threat that you now posed to my life and to my livelihood really blew my mind away.

For the next ten days I had to carry around a reminder that my body had allowed something that did not belong to us to come in and wreak havoc on my bladder. He said it was attached to my organ and I imagined it to be heavy and bothersome. But I tried with all of my might to not allow it to dissuade me from what I believed would be simply a mass.

On the tenth day as the doctor began telling me about you. I sat very still and stoic as I listened to him tell me that you were a 'high reactive cancer.' He stated matter-of-factly that I would have another procedure in a month to be sure that it was gone. I had to heal some before he began the next probe into my body to ensure there was no internal damage done to the rest of my organs. What caused me to regain focus was the doctor telling me that had I waited… the conversation and the outcome would be very different. As he spoke, I swear I was having an out-of-body experience. It was a good thing that I am a note taker because I would not have remembered anything that was said.

The doctor would ask several times if I understood what he was saying, and I told him I understood when in fact I simply wanted to run as far away from him and that office as fast as I could. To be honest I didn't want to understand. I did not want this thing to have an effect on me. I did not want the fear that comes with it.

Initially I didn't know how to feel so I was extremely quiet allowing my mind to catch up with the doctors' words. I kept hoping that maybe I heard him wrong, but all the signs indicated that this was my new reality. My mind was racing as fear sat at the edge of my pulse waiting to creep into my bones. I think I was on the verge of having a full fledge panic attack, but I couldn't dare fall apart. Falling apart is not allowed when you are the glue that holds others together. For the first time in a very long time I was afraid, and I could not think of anyone who could handle the weight of what I needed to share. So, I held it in and tried as best as I could to manage this new information and relied very heavily upon my faith to see me thru this new reality. At that moment though… I was spiraling out of control on the inside and I had every question imaginable, yet I had no real answers.

Out of all of the things that I had going on how did God think that this was what I needed at this point in my life? I don't know if I should have been angry, but I was. I didn't think it was fair even though I never doubted that He couldn't see me through it. But at that moment it felt extremely heavy. For weeks it felt like someone had sat a house on my shoulders and I was not sure I could balance that along with everything else happening. There were so many random thoughts that ran through my head. My initial reaction was to go into isolation but that was not possible. The next thought was to run away and live my best life without thought or reservation. Just go and possibly never look back; that wasn't an option either. I had to stay and navigate the days ahead that were unknown to me.

What I want to know more than anything is what gave you the right to start growing in my body? There was not even the subtlest of indication that you were there? The doctors didn't know either so where did you come from? You took full residence inside my bladder for God knows how long. You sat growing along the wall of my organ without any prior consent from me. You lived with me; you ate when I ate; you drank when I drank and existed as my tenant. While you threatened to take my life away, I had to take the utmost care to ensure you were evicted properly. I didn't like you at all and the resentment I felt for you was palpable. Who does that? What gave you the right to disrupt my life?

As I began the road to healing every thought possible ran thru my mind. Was it something that I could have done differently? Was this stress reimagined? Was this a result of the many times my heart has been broken. How could this happen to me and I am supposed to be healthy!! I tried not to get into my feelings about it because that would not help anything. But the human parts of me wanted to ball up and scream with abandon.

The one time I did finally break and allow myself to feel what was happening, I grieved for the feeling of helplessness that I felt since learning that you were there. I allowed the weight of it all to hit me and I sobbed because this time I couldn't fix it. I knew that in order to be one hundred percent again I would have to follow the doctor's orders and give myself the time my body needed to recover. I think that made me even angrier because I absolutely never got sick. There was not one real indication that there was something foreign happening.

Tumor what did you think you would gain by not making me aware? Did you think you would take me out? Although my initial reaction was shock and then disbelief I never once thought that you would win. Even though I knew there was a chance that there would be something to fight thru I never expected you.

I can tell you this… You will NOT win and whatever you thought you were going to accomplish won't happen! I am too strong and too formidable for you to destroy me.

Life happens for everyone and although I would not have ever imagined telling anyone that this would be my story. Yet there I was adjusting to this invasion recognizing that obviously I am not exempt from hardship. I believe that life prepared me however I didn't want any parts of it at all. So, I made the decision to use this to grow me to whatever the next level was for me. I knew that this would not destroy me, and it would not be the end.

It wasn't mine to begin with and I had no intentions to hold on to something that didn't belong to me.

* Has life ever thrown you a curve ball that literally knocked the wind out of you? Where did you find the strength to face the adversity?

The Truth I Didn't Tell...

"… Let patience have her perfect work they say."

11
BE PATIENT WITH ME

Dear Journal,

During one of the more difficult times in my life I found myself in search of answers. Everything seemed to be open ended and abrupt. I found myself slowly but surely losing control. I needed answers and they weren't coming. And here I was falling apart, and the anxiety was causing me to unravel at the seams. It was so unlike me to act erratic or not appear to be together, but I was a mess and there was nothing I could do about it.

Everything that could go wrong had gone wrong and here I was in this hurricane and it seems that He was no longer interested in my tantrums or me. I simply wanted to be sure of my next moves. I was finally tired of doing things my way. It did not seem unreasonable at the time but obviously God was not interested in moving any faster. What had I done to not hear anything? Moreover, didn't I deserve understanding and clarity?

God was the only one who could guide me out of this mess that I had gotten myself into. Even my friends who I enlisted to help me with my plight felt that it was not their place. That infuriated me because in the past I have tried to be there for everyone. Now it was my turn, and no one would even attempt to help me knowing that I wouldn't ask if I didn't really need it. Some I really trusted to be honest with me and instead I got a regurgitation of their own trauma.

This radial silence from God felt personal. I began to question everything that had ever happened in my life. Why did it seem that my junk was always life changing? I didn't have little trials… all of mine seemed to knock the wind out of me. I used to joke and say He was an 11:59 God; meaning He came at the last minute, in the last hour. I began to wonder why it seemed He always seemed to take His sweet time with me. I just wanted some relief and if He couldn't give me relief where was I supposed to get it?

I am certain the way I went about it was all wrong, but I was at my wits end. I literally was acting like a child who was determined to force the hand of my parent. There were times that I became almost belligerent yelling at Him in my head! I didn't want to be patient. I wanted direction and instead it felt like I was being stretched from one country to the next. Yet, the only thing I heard was "be patient." After repeatedly being told the same thing; "it will happen in my time and not yours" only added fuel to my angst.

I went to sleep one night angry at the lack of response and I guess God had enough of my antics and me. He awakened me with a stern "Get up!!" I got up and the same word was ringing in my head patience. But this time He commanded that I look up its meaning.

   Reluctantly I got up and I got my dictionary out of my office and looked up the word that I had begun to hate. And there it was written in black and white defying all that I thought patience was. It was uncomfortable at first to see the habits and actions that I thought I had overcome. More than that I had been commended of my patience in the past and to see that I still had some work to do made me feel like somewhat of a fraud. That was hard to swallow; even harder to digest.

   I became curious so I began to explore what the other references had to say to me as it relates to patience. I looked in the bible; the dictionary and thesaurus as well to see if they were all consistent. I needed to be sure that what God was conveying to me was real and not I trying to answer my own prayer.

   Dictionary.com defines patience like this:

> *"The ability to endure provocation annoyance, misfortune, or pain with calm & strength; an ability or willingness to suppress restlessness or annoyance when confronted with delay. The ability to have quiet, steady perseverance."*

   This wore me the rest of the way out because I sincerely thought I had patience before but to see this only let me know that I had more work to do.

Ironically, it seems that God is saying, "I Am Your God and you don't have the authority or the power to make me do anything! What you will do is wait until I think you can handle what I have promised you." Just like a child that has been told something great. The child becomes restless and cannot wait to see what is in store for him/her. Today I heard resounding in my spirit…"be anxious for nothing, but in everything through prayer and supplication with Thanksgiving let your requests be made known unto God…"

This right here should have been enough to comfort my discomfort but in my anxiousness, it exasperated my mental space because this was not in my control. I guess this was where I was supposed to admit that I might have had a control problem. That's hard to admit when I didn't know that being deliberate and intentional was a problem. As I sat and shook my head thinking of this conundrum that I found myself in; I could only ask that God would help me in my unbelief. I wanted to believe that God knew my character and He knows me, which is why this life lesson is one of the hardest for me to grasp. It was difficult because as a "fixer" I was supposed to not let anyone see me sweat… or hurt. I was supposed to have it all together and this realization made the cracks in my armor show. I was literally and physically holding on by a small fragment of thread.

Yes, I was supposed to hold up the promises of God in search of comfort during this pruning process. I know patience produces/yields experience and experience itself yields hope.

God now was asking me where was the hope (belief) that He could answer my prayer. It became how could you profess to others "God can do it!" Yet I didn't believe it myself.

I had to re-learn how to go through trials and tribulations. I had to remember how I got through some of the roughest periods of my life and apply those principals. Prayer, praise and worship had always been my posture and that's what I had to resort to instead of pouting and stomping my feet like a child.

Another lesson was that delay does not mean denial. Not because I will not receive it; but things happen when they are supposed to. They do not because I have been demanding results but because I have been patient with the process. There is a difference between faith believing and spirit demanding! I was guilty of wanting instant gratification.

In my own finite mind, I thought that immediately after all of these amazing revelations I would be granted pardon, a reprieve. Not the case. The lessons continued. Matter of fact I am still learning about patience and recognizing when I am being impatient. It's no easy feat allowing God to perfect the things in me that He knows will be beneficial to me later. I would like to say that He includes me on all of the decisions He makes for me; however, that is not the case at all...

So here I go trying to get this thing right so that I may be able to move forward with what God has for me... I surrender.

* Maybe patience was not the lesson you had to learn, but what trait or characteristic do you possess that had to be matured to a place that it benefitted you better?

_____
_____
_____
_____
_____
_____
_____
_____
_____
_____
_____
_____
_____
_____

The Truth I Didn't Tell...

"…It won't hurt they said… They lied!! It hurt like HELL!!"

12
LOVE...

Dear Journal,

I wrote an ode to love. Its disjointed as love often is. However, somehow it makes sense to the rhythm in which it flowed. How can something so meaningful be so complicated?

As a child I remember wanting to be picked to be a part of the team. I thought if I were chosen, I was accepted, and I belonged. Even then I wanted then to be a part of someone and something meaningful. Yet, its inevitable sting was poignant even then. I tell you this thing is so confusing and complicated... it's called love.

What is it this thing called Love? Sometimes it seems requited; other times not so much. Most times it feels misunderstood and understated. It's a language very few are fluid in, yet we all want to become versed in it. We desire to speak of its forbidden verses. Many of us hide from it, behind it but hiding nevertheless. I hate myself sometimes for wanting something that does not seem to want me. I have wondered if anyone else has felt that impression or longing to be desired. To want to be a part of something so bad that it hurts a long, dull throbbing pain as it courses its way through my veins. It is the kind of ache that you surely feel but there isn't a pain remedy that can cure its longing. Still we want what we do not know how to obtain. It is so powerful even when it sometimes leaves you powerless. How is that even possible?

For far too long, I longed for someone to really love me. Not with reason or rhyme but because I wanted to be special to someone and that someone made the choice to love me back. I have bought what I had hoped would be love only to find that the cost was my heart in the end. I gave myself freely expecting that it would be reciprocal, not knowing that I was never in their equation to begin with. Yet, the void remains the same. Desolate, distant, and empty…

I have heard and have read that we are to love our neighbors as ourselves. Well obviously, we haven't done a good job because we are a people projecting that same void and loneliness onto others. Although I do know what it feels like to be loved; I also know the cost of that love. I am in awe of the mystery behind a word that is so few in letters but vast in its meaning. What is this thing called love? Really?

Love can cause us to shut totally down; bury ourselves in a place of dark, damp, misery. Yet, we still seek after it like it is a drug that we have become addicted to. It is powerful, lucid, empowering, demoralizing, pure, corrupt, black, white, even purple in its character…it's all of these things? Yet, it is none of them for real. Oh, and do not forget red. It is definitely red!! What is love and where does its root stem from? Why is it imperative for survival?

I want to know! To scream for an answer! A reason! The cause! Frustration immediately comes to mind. Anger raises her hand screaming "DO NOT LEAVE ME OUT!" Unfortunately, sarcasm lives here too. It is as if the Gods are laughing hilariously at us as we try to simplify this obvious mystery of the great powerful thing that is small in nature.

I have read that love is patient and kind; slow to anger and to wrath. Are we fooling ourselves and it's a myth or are we just destined to play the game? Singers sing about it. Actors portray it. But who gets the award; the actors on stage or the ones who are living it every day?

I feel like I should've received an Academy Award for portraying happiness when my soul was hurting from having my heart broken repeatedly. I smiled to mask the discontentment in my soul and the hole where my heart used to live. I have held out hope that if I look content that maybe no one will notice the cracks in the masked facade.

*Is there a price too high for a love that changes your life?

The Truth I Didn't Tell...

"...I hear that a heart can't break because it is a muscle. If that's true why does my heart ache like this?!?"

13
BROKENHEARTED

Dear Journal,

Love is that thing that persons are born seeking and yearning for its place in life. Somehow it seems to be an innate force that requires energy and nurturing. Imagine though an entire life not knowing or feeling that you are deserving of love and its first appearance is a semblance of the real thing. However, his or her love was not available to be given because it already belonged to someone else. What we shared were stolen moments that attempted to give me value and need. That experience left me with my heart shattered and my first seed lying lifeless in a cold machine; its life taken before I was able to experience unconditional love.

No one knew of that first heartbreak because I put it next to the mantle of pain that I had built inside my heart where all of the other hurts lived. In true fashion I pushed past it and picked up more shifts at work so as not to "feel" that empty feeling of helplessness.

I tried my hand at a presentation of love over and over; again and again until I realized that what I needed and what they wanted were two very different things. My heart was never factored into the many equations yet because of my thirst for a love that was requited I believed and kept hoping. Time and time again I put my heart on the line in hopes of fixing their damaged pieces so they could fit the damaged places in my own life. I finally deduced that it had to be me, and they simply didn't want all of me. They only wanted what they needed to fill the void at that moment… my body. Their needs were not mine and my needs were not theirs. I remained hungry for the attention and longing for the gentle touch of someone that wasn't raising their hand in anger… I kept trying.

Here I was vulnerable and naive hoping that someone would add value to the broken pieces that were left from so much trauma. It was too much weight to impose upon someone especially when they didn't know that my expectation was for them to restore my hope in love. The complete irony of this was that I wasn't even aware of the previous damages that had been done. I had become a master of disguise; I knew how to dress it up and make it look good. I learned very early how to manage the bruises without bringing attention to myself.

Unfortunately, as I continued to grow the bruising was now invisible to the human eye because they were not motivated by fists but were now emotionally stimulated.

After many failed attempts at what I thought was love and what I later viewed as attempts to right the wrongs of my past; I finally had enough. I began to take a real assessment of what my needs were. I took note of each person that took advantage of my vulnerable self and I had to see the parts that I also played. There were instances for sure where I was intrigued with an individual and I wanted to try to make it work. Even when the flags were bright red and waving hysterically in my mind "that this is not it!!!" Yet I kept trying; hoping; needing to believe that somehow that this time it would not end up just like the others… another failed attempt at love.

I had been accused of being a hopeless romantic and a person who could be somewhat gullible. There was maybe some truth to it; however, I wasn't ready to admit that as much as I was ready to end the cycle. I no longer wanted the empty promises and the nights that turned into mornings of regret. I wanted something that was tangible and real. Even when my heart told me that it was no longer going along with my shenanigans I still somehow believed in love.

For what seemed like forever; I kept meeting the same type of persons. They were either broken; damaged; battered or had severe trust issues. They were obviously damaged from previous relationships and I felt it was my duty to fix them. I took on many meaningless projects that amounted to more heartbreak and disappointment. I had grown exasperated with the entire process.

One day I was blindsided by love and it knocked the literal wind out of me. I had warded off the idea of love and its empty promises. I will never forget the day that my heart raced throughout the entire first conversation. I hung up my phone and walked away shaking my head in disbelief. I learned that we had so many things in common and so many interests. I asked myself, "This could not possibly be true… right?" My disbelief came because my heart was very fragile, and I was terrified of what would happen if I were left destroyed from this new interest. It took months for me to own the fact that I was falling in love. Out of my fear I began the retreat within myself in an effort to protect my heart from what I felt would be the inevitable.

Our relationship began just as I had always dreamt that real love would. It was majestic and beautiful. Days turned into nights and mornings into evenings of pure bliss. I fell hopelessly down the spiral before I knew it and I became deathly afraid of what would happen if I allowed this reckless abandon to continue. Unbeknownst to me they too were falling in love; the thing is neither of us was prepared for what would happen when we emerged out of the bubble. We never took the time to do the hard work that it required to manage the type of love that we were building. We wanted the dream sincerely and together we had such amazing chemistry; yet we failed to prepare for the reality of life.

Eventually one of us was confronted with something that reminded us of a trauma that was capable of destroying us. Life happened and eventually it did just that… slowly it began to unravel. I tried as I might to brace my heart for the inevitable but there was nothing to prepare me.

My heart finally broke into a million pieces and there I was emotionally devastated. I sincerely felt like there was no way I could hurt any more than I did at that moment. At times I felt like God hated me and that my heart could no longer ignore pain of the dull ache that had replaced my heartbeat. My heart broke into the bottle of vodka that no longer numbed the pain and the tears that accompanied that ache seemed to end at the beginning of the next ones. I lost myself in an abyss of heartache for months existing only long enough to show up for things that were necessary. Then it was a quick return back to my seat of heartbreak. I don't know how long I sat there waiting for life to make sense or my heart to simply stop.

It never stopped and that proved to me that there was more to live for. I had to really do some soul work to get back to a place of wellness. It was also necessary to accept that while I hated the absence of that love, it was necessary to be grateful for the beauty that I experienced as a result of that love.

One day I woke up and I decided that I no longer wanted to be a victim. What I wanted to experience and needed was already inside and I had to trust me again… to trust love again. It was time to gamble on me.

I took as much time as needed to do the work needed for my healing. There were many days of doubt and even more days of realization that it was up to me to change this narrative. I had to realize that everything that I had experienced was my classroom. I was supposed to be in every situation. I was being equipped for something greater... even love. What I knew for sure was that I didn't have to be Superman anymore. The only person I had to prove something to was me. I simply had to be me and be better than good with me. That's the day I began to live by learning to love me better than anyone else was capable of. I was alive and while it was no accident; I had to live on purpose and intentionally.

* Are you willing to risk it all for a love that may not be able to catch you as deeply as you fall?

Recondius Obrien

"… Spirits shifts; Mind shifts; Uncomfortable… Growth."

14
GROWING PAINS

Dear Journal,

The seasons were changing, and the leaves had turned into beautiful hues of brown, red, yellow, and orange. People were hustling and bustling to their various destinations with purposed strides and sure steps. Most were consumed with where they were destined and not necessarily the route traveled to get there. Others meandered along flowing with the breeze and crisp of the winter air. It was December and 2008 was moving hastily to a close. There was one thing that I noticed as I people watched and observed the actions of my fellow man and women. There had to have been a lot of love making during the spring and summer of '08 because folks were pregnant and having babies! I assumed since the nation stated that we were in a recession (according to the reports) that they would stay in and find solace in the folds or confines of one another.

Myself being a man and technically unable to "bear" children per se it makes me ponder. What would it feel like to be pregnant and the idea of life is about to come forth through you? What are the thoughts of someone at the pivotal point in their lives? How difficult is it to wrap your mind and arms around the idea that you will be responsible for someone quite possibly for the rest of their lives? Do any of the responsibilities come to mind along with the reality that after nine months you will have a child that began as a seed. Since I cannot possibly imagine the mental and physical endurance that it requires to actually go through labor... Allow me to challenge your thought process briefly while I try to reason with this thing called "pregnancy" and the actual delivery of the "life" that is "carried" in your womb.

Webster defines pregnancy as:

> *"the period between conception and birth when a woman carries a fetus in her womb."*

Knowing that to be impregnated with something means that there had to be a conception. I am inclined to believe that (although one may refute my approach) we (humans) can also become pregnant with ideas, purpose, and life. Question is... what needs to happen so that we don't miscarry our ideas? How long can a thought be given to become a great idea? It is very possible to lose hope and abort because of the vastness of the idea and what it may take to "birth" these new ideas. And it is safe to say that challenges have to be considered. Let's talk about that fact that the idea seems out of this world yet, you hesitated to share it with anyone because you did not want to be misunderstood. Support is everything when you are considering something that is bigger than you. Oftentimes that can be the death of an idea.

Many of us have had ideas that we knew could change the world. Yet, because your vision seemed much bigger than you planned, and your friends don't get it can cause abandonment of an idea. That's when the thought of it failing becomes larger than life and accountability becomes real. Additionally, I can imagine that after so many failed attempts in the past, it could make anyone afraid to believe in the impossible. Life is not always per se the breath of a being, but life is the breath of an idea and what we do with it.

I realize that for some it may be wayyy too far left to absorb but what if we are impregnated with new ideas that will pivot us for the next level in our lives? What if the next promotion is outside of the comfort zones? If the goal is to win, we must learn to accept the challenges that can move us to where we want to be. There are some circumstances that may cause one to become weary, tired, overwhelmed and it's in those times that you have to simply regroup and refocus. We still have to consider even in the planning period that it takes time for greatness to come. It just does not happen overnight. You have to plan to be great and work the plan no matter how long the process takes.

I know for a fact 2008 was a year of completion for me and I was eagerly anticipating the New Year. There is something about the ability to start anew and push the reset button that was ideal for me. I was not ready to run away from my ideas; quite the contrary I felt like I was almost ready to bring all of my ideas to fruition. The newness was bubbling up inside me and I wanted to embrace all of these thoughts that I wanted to bring to reality. I was so excited that I had not given up when things became hard. It was hard and sometimes arduous trying to finish school and stay committed to all of the things that I was responsible for. Yet, I still believed that every idea that I had inside of me would become a tangible reality.

God entrusted me with the thoughts that became ideas and He allowed them to take root in my spirit at the start of 2008. I will be the first to tell you that there were days when I wanted to run like hell and get away from all of the thoughts that were threatening to manifest in my heart and mind. Suddenly it became real and possible; to be honest it was sometimes frightening.

There were times when I felt I should just stop trying to reach that next level for my life, but I didn't want to abandon the things that had been sown in my spirit. I happen to believe that great ideas are born out of the barrenness within our minds. The bible states clearly that, "According to the power that works in me, that I have the ability to obtain wealth!" now I may be reading more into it but I believe that whatever 'it' is i.e. wealth, good health, a new business, a mate, whatever it is that I desire of God… He is faithful and just to perform it.

We cannot allow past hurts, incidents, and misfortunes to sidetrack us. We have to carry these precious ideas to fruition simply because giving up is not an option. Find the reasoning that lead you to believe you could in the first place just as I have repeatedly. It actually hurts (much like I think labor may feel like) before it becomes reality but trust me, it will become bearable if you don't give up on it. Your ideas morph into life when you actually realize its potential and begin nurturing them. Failure only becomes an option when you decide that you no longer want to fuel your dreams. There is a place deep inside you that will allow the process to become synonymous with purpose. You have to think about everything that you had to endure to get to this point and while the process is oftentimes long you will be made better for it. I am speaking from experience and all of the effort will be worth it.

There will even be times when others will question your why but that is not yours to manage. It is up to you to know your why. That why is what you need as fuel in order to see your desires through? In the times of doubt, I had to rely on something greater and more powerful to lift me and so will you. That's the only way you can survive growing pains. Allow the madness to push you all the way to your new life, that new idea, surely that new way of thinking! Fuel your mind with ideas of success and see yourself at the finish line. Your mind is fresh soil and it should be nourished and nurtured with support and good energy. It is not anyone else's responsibility to fulfill our purpose in life. It is however up to us to give birth to our purpose and create new and fresh ideas that carry the possibility to change the world.

* Is there one idea that you abandoned because you did not believe that you have the capacity to bring it to fruition?

"… From the caterpillar to the cocoon…
to emergence. Please let me go!"

15
FREE

Dear Journal,

I wrote this piece in an effort to express my need to be free from the confines of others as well as the confines within my mind. I simply want to be...

I am the Butterfly escaping the grasps of my cocoon

I am an eagle soaring above the threatening abyss below

I am the ruler of my destiny because He told me I could be...

I am Free

I am the crystal liquid cascading over the edges of Niagara's fall

I am the molten lava morphing into the folds of smoldering volcanoes

I, you see am the everlasting threat to bondage!

I am Free

Free as my ancestors were when they danced their way out of slavery

Into the fields of freedom

Free as the hands & chains that bound me; wishing they were free as me

Free to overcome the adversity that was designed to cripple me

Damn, I am that free

Free to explore the possibility of possible

Free to not be afraid of the impossible

Free to allow the wind to separate every strand of the curly fro on my head

Simply Free

I exhale; I breathe; I stretch; Finally, I am…

FREE TO JUST… BE NO ONE ELSE
BUT ESPECIALLY ME.

"Tonight, I feel like I need to release every care and let my hair down; that's exactly what I planned to do!!"

— circa 1995

16
BLUES DANCING

Dear Journal,

As I walked into the venue, I had one objective in my head...that was to dance until I felt the earth move and all of my cares were memories. All I needed was a strong bass beat that would cause my rhythm to move me to freedom. I somehow knew if I could just get to the dimly illuminated dance floor, I could be free. The cool, black floor looked like an oasis of black water beckoning me to cast my cares into the abyss of its depth. I stood in awe momentarily of its beauty as I awaited the chord that would pull me into its current, allowing me to shake, gyrate and exorcise myself loose. I wanted to be one with the music so much so that we flowed effortlessly into each other. I did not want to think of how it looked. Honestly, I didn't even care. I, for once was going to be free of the eyes of judgment and just be. All I wanted was to liberate myself into a whole 'nother stratosphere. I feared that I had become a prisoner within me... lost in the body of my own self; this was going to serve as my coming out period.

For the next few hours I wanted to not think and not care about what happened outside of the music. I simply wanted to dance...

See then when I danced it would speak volumes without ever saying an audible world. Yet, even then if not careful it told my story. This time I wasn't so much concerned with telling the story as I was with writing it... new chapter(s) free and carefree. This chapter did not require me to be so damn predictable. I know it doesn't make sense to want to abandon the cares of the world (if only for a moment) but I had become the master illusionist. When the need to escape the pressures became too severe I could see myself dancing free. Losing myself in the sway of the rhythm as I danced. Dancing in a way that would tell a story with intrinsically woken lines and deep creases of life without me disclosing too much. It gave me permission to be human.

There were internal screams that if audible would awaken the dead; guttural sounds that ached to be released; tongues that rambled without distinction but totally inappropriate for delicate souls needing understanding. I, however, heard the muted groaning and moaning desiring to be freed and became one with them.

All the while there remains this feeling down in my soul pulling me to release all that held me captive. A rhythm down in the innermost parts of my being, propelling me to feel the current running underneath my skin proving that there is still push inside of me... moreover life.

The Truth I Didn't Tell...

There is a beat capable of moving my soul and carrying me to a land of melodies and choruses, lines, extensions and bass lines. The need to ease onto the dance floor and exorcise the rumblings of sorts inside my being with fierceness that Ailey would be proud of doesn't escape me. This longing to become one with the rhythm and the blues of dance stirs the fibers of my soul.

This dance indicates that there is something or someone captive breaking free, dancing for the essence of expression. The conversations being held with my limbs beckon my being to react; jolt on the inner, causing the outers of me to quake uncontrollably. I try to control the fire but I can't; its current coursing through me trying to win. Not that I do not want to release it, but I am afraid of what may happen if I set loose the frustrations and anxieties that I have suppressed for so long.

That's the thing about the blues and its power(s). It can singe your soul and strain your heart. And when released it paints a picture that the world will see as different or perverted. It's an art that gracefully emerges from the throes of an artist; an art that suggests that there is a story behind the obvious lines and strokes.

I remember oh so well being guided by the deejay into a trance as I began to create my own personal masterpiece. I can feel the energy as I think of the nights I spent making art, creating the script for my seemingly meaningless life. I became my destiny on those nights so much so I allowed my spirit to take over my body. My spirit would lead me onto the edge of the dance floor stomping, spinning, and gyrating until the tears fell from my eyes freeing me from the bondages of life. I danced 'til all the brokenness of my life became a whole memory. I danced every passed over hurt and rejection away! I danced until I became numb and the essence of feeling no longer existed. I danced until the crowd thinned to leave so my soul and me were free to finally soar through the air to dance effortlessly. My clothes became a soaking wet mass as they stuck to my scorched skin. My hair became limp and stringy as I tried to shake off every dead thing that held me captive. I was the "blues dancing."

Once again, I long to become the rhythm and be free like that again. I want to rediscover where I misplaced the blues so that I may find the melody and the beat of my fears. I wonder if it would still call out to the very core of my being; and beg for acknowledgement as it did then. I still desire to dance all of my cares away, dance until my already tired limbs ache. Dance until freedom becomes liberation. Dance through the woes and the stresses; the cares and the pressures. Dance till my eyes pour freely the tears withheld because I just couldn't let them go. I want to feel that light, take flight airy feeling that you feel when you have become one with the spirit. Dance until…just whenever the "spirit" lifts. The ability to dance a soul cleansing; spiritual dance that celebrates the freedom from bondage and the shackles of life is so freeing. That's how I want to express my blues and the dance that comes from it.

Blues dancing…. That's me arms flailing, head banging, hips swaying, toe curling, life changing, soul freeing dance…

*Dancing was always my way to release. Have you found an outlet that safely allows you to be uninhibited and free?

The Truth I Didn't Tell...

ABOUT THE AUTHOR

Recondius Obrien is an Author; Life Coach and International Speaker. He has lectured in many of our 50 states. His gifts lie in excavating the unique rare beauty that is often overlooked.

While his travels are vast he has had to rely on his inner strengths in an effort to discover the truths that weren't told.

It is because of his personal journey with this discovery that maybe there were others who struggled with their own truths.

This book was birthed as a response to the calling of the others who didn't have a voice. Here you will find the keys and the signed permission slip to live and be your authentic self.

In this new freedom Recondius Obrien enjoys crafting culinary delights, sketching, interior design and all things creative.

To learn more and to connect with the author go to www.theoexperience.com

CPSIA information can be obtained
at www.ICGtesting.com
Printed in the USA
FSHW020842080321
79179FS